SPANISH BALLADS

Also by W.S. Merwin

Unframed Originals: Recollections, 1982
Houses and Travellers, 1977
The Miner's Pale Children, 1970

TRANSLATIONS

Sir Gawain & the Green Knight, 2002
Purgatorio, 2000
East Window: The Asian Translations, 1998
Pieces of Shadow: Selected Poems of Jaime Sabines, 1996
Sun at Midnight (Poems by Musō Soseki) (with Soiku Shigematsu), 1989
Vertical Poetry (Poems by Roberto Juarroz), 1988
From the Spanish Morning, 1985
Four French Plays, 1985
Selected Translations 1968–1978, 1979
Euripedes' Iphigeneia at Aulis (with George E. Dimock Jr.), 1978
Osip Mandelstam: Selected Poems (with Clarence Brown), 1974
Asian Figures, 1973
Transparence of the World (Poems by Jean Follain), 1969, 2003
Voices (Poems by Antonio Porchia), 1969, 1988, 2003
Products of the Perfected Civilization (Selected Writings of Chamfort), 1969
Twenty Love Poems and a Song of Despair (Poems by Pablo Neruda), 1969
Selected Translations 1948–1968, 1968
The Song of Roland, 1963
Lazarillo de Tormes, 1962
Spanish Ballads, 1961, 2008
The Satires of Persius, 1960
The Poem of the Cid, 1959

ANTHOLOGY

Lament for the Makers: A Memorial Anthology, 1996

Spanish Ballads

Translated with a new Foreword by

W.S. MERWIN

Copper Canyon Press

Port Townsend, Washington

Cover photo: Valerie Brewster

Originally published as a hardcover edition, *Some Spanish Ballads* (Abelard-Schuman, Limited, 1961), and as a softcover *Spanish Ballads* (Doubleday, 1961).

Copper Canyon Press is in residence at Fort Worden State Park in Port Townsend, Washington, under the auspices of Centrum. Centrum is a gathering place for artists and creative thinkers from around the world, students of all ages and backgrounds, and audiences seeking extraordinary cultural enrichment.

LIBRARY OF CONGRESS CATALOGING-IN-PUBLICATION DATA

Spanish ballads / translated with an Introduction by W.S. Merwin.

p. cm.

Includes bibliographical references.

ISBN 978-1-55659-278-2 (pbk.: alk. paper)

1. Ballads, Spanish—Spain—Translations into English.

2. Spanish poetry—Translations into English.

I. Merwin, W. S. (William Stanley), 1927- II. Title.

PQ6267.E4B28   2008

861'.04408 — dc22

2008004200

3 5 7 9 8 6 4 2

FIRST PRINTING

COPPER CANYON PRESS

Post Office Box 271

Port Townsend, Washington 98368

www.coppercanyonpress.org

For Sylvia Plath and Ted Hughes

Contents

Foreword

This book of translations dates from my youth, though from a time when my youth, in a sense, was coming to an end. Francois Villon, in "l'an trentiesme de mon age" (the thirtieth year of my age), considered his youth to be over — and probably most of his life as well. Pound quoted that line in a vivid sequence of poems written at more or less that age. I had the poetry of both of them in my ear long before I turned thirty. Pound the poet and translator had influenced my way of hearing poetry ever since I discovered *Personae*, his first collection of selected poems, in a small college-town bookshop when I was around eighteen, and by then I was trying to learn French and Old French well enough to be able to read Villon in the original.

I had even made a few clumsy attempts at translating poems by that time. My Spanish professor, a young man in a beret who went everywhere on bicycle and was profoundly homesick for Spain, needed some help in translating Lorca's poems, many of which he knew by heart. When he found out that I was trying to write poetry myself he asked me to help him, and others from his small class volunteered to help translate one of Lorca's late plays. And so the first book of twentieth-century poetry I read was Lorca's *Romancero gitano*. I was already under the spell of medieval poetry, led to it by Villon, and was struggling to make sense of Old French and to hear something in the old poems that I might recognize as poetry.

After reading Pound's translations, and the handful of beautiful translations by John Peale Bishop that are now undeservedly forgotten and include two very lyrical versions of troubadour poems, I managed to turn out a brocade-stiff English rendition of Richard Coeur de Lion's famous prison song, without even realizing that it was a real troubadour poem or that Richard's great-grandfather had been the Guilhem IX, Duc d'Aquitaine, Lo Coms de Peiteus, "the first troubadour."

In the spring of 1948, when I was twenty, I went to see Pound in Washington, DC, where he was locked up in a psychiatric ward of St. Elizabeths Hospital. He was in there for his own good. He had been living in Europe for the greater part of his life, mostly in Italy, where U.S. troops, advancing northward late in World War II, had arrested him. He was still an American citizen and he had made propaganda speeches on the Italian radio in support of Mussolini during wartime. He was charged with treason. His prosecutors wanted him shot, and his defense attorneys had made use of an insanity plea to save him. Someone at the time is reported to have asked T.S. Eliot, Pound's friend for many years, whether Pound "was really crazy," and Eliot is said to have answered, "Well, you know Ezra."

I didn't, of course, and I had yet to be confronted by the full awfulness of Pound's politics and his racism. His insistence on trying "to resuscitate the dead art / Of poetry; to maintain 'the sublime' / In the old sense," and something that I had heard here and there in his poems, had made him a hero to me. It would not be long before I was forced to recognize the appalling nature of some of his persistent views, which must have been aired on the Italian fascist radio and which recurred in many passages of his cantos. The recognition of them turned Pound, for me, as for other poets and readers from Pound's generation to the present, into a troubling enigma. He is someone to whom many of us know we are indebted but whose opinions, and the character that could have maintained them, we find intolerable.

But I had not yet had to face that, when I went to visit him in St. Elizabeths Hospital. When I met him he seemed to take me seriously, as a young man bent on writing poetry. He told me, in his authoritative way, that I ought to write "about seventy-five lines a day" and that since, at my age, I had nothing to write about, the only way to do that was to translate. I should translate anyway, as a method of exploring what I could do with my own language. And I should try to "get as close to the original as possible," which sounded like a simple goal until I began to try to put it into practice and to wonder exactly what it meant.

It was not the only valuable nugget of advice that Pound handed me on that visit. I was in awe of him and it rendered me incapable of recognizing how dearly he loved to propound, to speak *ex cathedra*. Gertrude Stein, as I would read before long, had described him as "a village explainer," which was all right "if you were a village." But some of what he said on that visit continued to encourage my own efforts. He urged me to learn languages "so that I would not be at the mercy of translators," for example. And he advised me to "get" what he called "the Provencal," the language of the troubadours, because it was they who began at the place where poetry and music were inseparable. When I told him that I had been studying Spanish for several years he said that the *Romancero* would be a useful place for me to start, for the time being.

I went back to college and took out of the library a large edition of the Spanish *Romancero*. I leafed through it, settling at random—as though the pieces were all of equal magic—on a poem that began "Descolorida zagala," and started to flounder over some way of conjuring into English something of what I thought must be the clear, ringing notes of the original—though in fact I could not hear anything of the kind in the Spanish. The literal sense of the words was no help. *Zagala* was just "maiden," a word already long out of colloquial use in English, a small receding cloud. As for *descolorida,* it meant "faded," "washed-out," "color-less." "Wan" would probably be the most reasonable word, in the circumstances. "Wan maiden" indeed sounded pretty washed out. No magic there. I felt sure that there must be some, just out of earshot in English, which I could summon with sheer attention and patience if only I could learn how to do it. It was a while before it struck me that the originals were in fact potted up in their own conventions, and that some of them were listless and ordinary. It was a lesson in choosing what to try to translate to begin with. To pick things I wanted to hear in English before even considering whether anything of the kind was imaginable.

I went on practicing with the *romances* for a while, though none of my efforts came to much. But I grew familiar with many of them and had favorites. When I was in my midtwenties, living in Mallorca after a time in London, the BBC Third Programme commissioned me to make a verse translation of the great medieval Spanish saga *El cantar del mio cid,* which was the narrative source of some of the oldest *romances.* As I worked on that I went back over some of the ones that were already familiar, and gradually I began to hear something, however distant, of the music of the ancient epic and its descendants.

Yet it was several more years before I tried again to translate the *romances* themselves. By that time I was living in London and had reached a turning point in my own writing. I was reading modern poetry in every language available to me, and translations from oral traditions wherever I could find them. The present collection is what I managed to make of them then.

I hope these translations convey something of what, by that time, I heard in the originals, and thought was worth trying to suggest in English, something that would be worth listening to and remembering.

W.S. Merwin
January 2008

SPANISH BALLADS

1. *Romances* from the Epic Cycles

La Cava Florinda's Fatal Immodesty

With gaiety and delight
La Cava and her maidens
Went out from a tower of the palace
By a postern gate
And made their way to a garden
Close to a dense grove
Of jasmines and myrtle trees
Grown in tangles and thickets.
Beside a fountain which spilled
Crystal and echoing pearls
From six spouts of fine gold
Among bulrushes and lilies,
The maidens took their ease
Seeking comfort and relief
From the fire of their youth
And the heat of summer.
They gave their arms to the water,
And, by its coldness tempted,
La Cava was the first
Who cast off her clothes.
In the shadowy pool
So fair her body shone
That, like the sun,
She eclipsed all others there.
She thought that she and her maidens

Were alone, but as it happened,
Through the dense ivy
King Rodrigo was watching.
And that moment kindled
Fire in his proud heart,
And love, with beating wings,
Inflamed him without warning.
This was the luckless beginning
Which brought on the loss of Spain:
An unlucky woman
And a man given up to love.
Florinda lost her flower,
The King suffered his punishment;
She said he forced her to it,
He said she gave full consent.
As for which of those two
Was more blameworthy,
Men will tell you it was La Cava,
And women, Rodrigo.

The Dream of King Don Rodrigo

The winds were roused,
The moon was at full,
The fishes made wailing cries
At the wild weather
While the good King Don Rodrigo
Slept beside La Cava
In a sumptuous tent
Adorned with gold all over.
Three hundred ropes of silver
Were what held it there,
Within were a hundred maidens
In wonderful apparel,
Fifty playing instruments
With marvelous accord,
Fifty of them singing
To a sweet air.
Then spoke a maiden,
Fortune was her name:
"King Don Rodrigo,
If you sleep, wake, I pray you,
And you will see your sad fate
And your worse ending,
And behold your people dead
And your army routed
And your towns and cities

In one day destroyed,
Your castles, fortresses,
Ruled by another lord.
Ask me who has done this,
I will tell you plainly:
Count Don Julián,
Out of love for his daughter,
Because you dishonored her
And she was all he had;
He has sworn an oath
Which will cost you your life."
He awoke in great anguish
At the sound of that voice;
With sad and woeful face
Thus he replied:
"Fortune, for your message
I am grateful to you."
At that moment there arrived
One who brought tidings
That the Count Don Julián
Was laying waste the lands.
He calls at once for his horse
And rides forth to meet him;
So many are his foes
That his courage avails nothing;
His captains and soldiers flee,
Each one as he can.

The Defeat of King Don Rodrigo

The hosts of Don Rodrigo
Took panic and fled.
In the eighth battle
His enemies conquered.
Rodrigo leaves his tents
And goes from the kingdom,
Alone in his wretchedness
He rides with no company,
His horse for weariness
Can scarcely go forward,
It wanders at its will;
He does nothing to guide it.
So faint is the King
That his senses are numb,
Dead with thirst and hunger,
Woeful to behold;
So red with blood,
He looks like a live coal.
His weapons are hacked,
That were crusted with jewels,
His sword like a saw-blade
With the blows it had taken,
His helmet so battered
It had sunk down on his head,

His face swollen
With the ordeal he had suffered.
   He comes to the top of a hill,
The highest one in sight,
From there he beholds his people
Fleeing in defeat,
From there he sees his banners
And the standards that once were his
Trampled into the earth
Till the ground covers them,
He looks for his captains
But none is to be seen,
He sees the field red with blood
Running off in rivers.
The wretched man, at the sight,
Is overcome with grief,
And weeping from his eyes
In this manner he speaks:
"Yesterday I was King of Spain,
Today not of one village;
Yesterday I had towns and castles,
Today I have not one;
Yesterday I had servants
And people to wait upon me;
Today there is not a battlement
Which I can call my own.
Ill-fated was the hour
And the day luckless

When I was born and fell heir
To so great a heritage
Since I was to lose it
In one day, all together!
Why do you not come, Death,
And take this soul of mine
From this wretched body
Which would be grateful to you?"

The Penance of King Don Rodrigo

King Don Rodrigo
When he had lost Spain
Departed in despair,
Fleeing from his ill fortune;
The luckless man went alone,
Wanting no company,
But the pain of Death
Followed close behind him.
He took his way to the mountains
Where they looked most forbidding.
He happened upon a shepherd
Who was herding his flock;
He said to him: "Good man,
Answer me this:
Are there churchmen nearby,
Or is there a monastery?"
Then the shepherd answered
That none such would he find
For in all that wilderness
There was no one but a hermit
In a hermitage
Living a holy life.
When he heard this the King was happy
To think he might end his life there;
He asked the shepherd to give him

Food, if he had any,
For the strength of his body
Was deserting him utterly.
The shepherd brought out a bag
Where he kept his bread,
He gave some to the King, and some salt beef
Which he happened to have there.
It was very black, that bread;
The King found it bitter;
Tears rose into his eyes,
He could not check them,
When he thought of all the things
That he had tasted in his lifetime.
When he had rested he asked
The way to the hermitage;
The shepherd showed it to him,
So that he should not be lost.
The King gave him a chain
And a ring which he had with him,
Jewels of great price
Which the King had treasured.
He set out on his way.
As the sun was sinking
He came to the hermitage
At the top of the mountains.
He found the hermit,
Who was more than a hundred years old.
"I am the wretched Rodrigo

Who at one time was king,
Who, by love led astray,
Has forfeited his soul,
And for whose black sins
All Spain lies in ruins.
In God's name, hermit, I beg you,
And in the name of Santa María,
To hear my confession,
For I wish for my life to end."
The hermit was filled with alarm
And answered him, in tears:
"I will hear your confession,
But I cannot absolve you."
When he had spoken these words
They heard a voice from heaven:
"Absolve him, confessor,
Upon your life absolve him,
And in his own tomb
Give him a penance."
As it was revealed to him,
The King carried it out:
He laid himself in the tomb
By the side of the hermitage;
In it there slept a serpent,
It was horrible to behold;
Three times round the tomb it was coiled;
It had seven heads.
"Offer prayers for me, hermit,

That I may end my life well."
The hermit spoke words of courage,
Then covered him with the tombstone.
Beside it, he prayed to God
All the hours of the day.
"Penitent, how fares it with you,
With your strong companion?"
"Now he is gnawing me, gnawing me
Where I most sinned,
He is gnawing straight into my heart,
The fount of my great misfortune."
The little bells of heaven
Resound with joy;
The bells of the earth
Rang out by themselves;
The soul of the penitent
Ascended into heaven.

The Birth of Bernardo del Carpio

Alfonso the Chaste was reigning
In the kingdom of León;
He had a beautiful sister,
Doña Jimena was her name.
None other than the Count of Saldaña
Fell in love with her,
And his love prospered, for the princess
Loved him in return.
Many times they were together
And no one suspected,
And from their many meetings
She went with child;
She brought forth a baby,
He was milk-white and scarlet,
They named him Bernardo
For his luckless fate;
While she was swaddling him
She bathed him in tears:
"Why were you ever born, son,
To so hapless a mother?
To me and to your father
You spell love and disgrace."
When the good king heard of it

He shut her up in a cloister,
And had the Count imprisoned
In Luna of the Towers.

Bernardo del Carpio Learns of His Father

In the court of Alfonso the Chaste
Bernardo lived at his pleasure,
Ignorant of the prison
Where his father was lying;
At this many were filled with sadness
But none told him the truth
Because the king had forbidden
Any mention of the thing.
Two ladies revealed it to him
Artfully and with cunning.
When Bernardo knew the truth
The blood soured in his veins;
Going out from where he was dwelling
He cried aloud his grief;
He dressed himself in black clothes
And went before the king.
Seeing him dressed in mourning,
The king spoke in this fashion:
"Can it be, Bernardo,
That you desire my death?"
Bernardo said: "My lord,
Your death I do not desire,
But I grieve for my father
Who has been this long time in prison.
I crave your mercy, good king,

May it be granted this day."
Alfonso was seized with wrath
And answered him in anger:
"Go from my sight, Bernardo,
And never again be so bold
As to speak to me of this
Or it will be the worse for you.
And I swear to you, I promise,
That for as long as I live
Not for one single day
Will your father leave that prison."
"My lord, you are king, you can do
As you please and as it suits you,
But you reward ill those who serve you
And would serve you still.
May God bestir your heart
Before long to release my father,
For I shall go in mourning
Until the day he is free."

The Complaint of the Count of Saldaña

The Count Don Sancho Díaz,
That lord of Saldaña,
Drenched are the prison walls
With the tears he sheds.
In his grief and solitude
He bewails his fortune
To his son Don Bernardo,
To Alfonso the King and his sister:
"These my sorrowful white hairs
Again and again remind me
Of the cheerless endless years
That I have passed in prison.
When I came into this castle
My beard was scarcely begun,
And now, for my transgressions,
I behold it long and white.
What neglect, my son!
How is it that my blood
Does not cry out in your veins
To lend help where it is needed?
No doubt you are detained
In your mother's footsteps,
And, being of the King's cause,
You must think ill of mine.
You are all three against me;

It is not enough for a wretch
To have such enemies,
He must have his own flesh turn against him.
All those who keep me here
Recount your deeds to me;
For whom do you amass honor
If not for your father?
Here I remain in these irons,
Since you do not set me free;
Either I am a bad father
Or you a bad son, to fail me.
If I offend you, forgive me,
For in words I find some relief,
For I shed tears, being old,
And you are silent, being absent."

First *Romance* of the Seven Princes of Lara

Now Castilians in anger
Ride out of Castile
To carry war to the walls
Of ancient Calatrava;
They smashed them in three places
Along the Guadiana;
Through one breach the Christians enter,
The Moors escape through the others
With curses for Mohammed
And his unholy sect,
And they flee with loud shrieks
High into the mountains.
Oh God, what a warrior
Was Rodrigo de Lara, that day!
For he killed five thousand Moors
And took three hundred captive.
If he had died at that time
What fame he would have left!
He would not have slain his nephews
The seven Princes of Lara,
He would not have sold their heads
To a Moor to take away.
Ruy Velazquez de Lara
Fought well on that day;
A rich tent from Arabia

And a bench of gold were his booty;
He sent them as a present
To the Count Garci Fernandez,
For him to arrange a marriage
With the fair Doña Lambra.
Now the wedding has been contracted
(Oh God, in an evil hour)
Between Doña Lambra de Bureba
And Don Rodrigo de Lara.
They held the marriage in Burgos
And the next day's feast in Salas;
At the wedding and the feasting
They spent seven weeks.
Well enough went the wedding
But not the feasting after.
They had summoned guests from Castile,
From León and from Navarre;
They came in such multitudes
That the lodgings could not contain them,
And the seven Princes of Lara
Had not yet arrived.
There, look there, they are coming
Across that level plain!
Their mother Doña Sancha
Rode out to receive them;
They kissed her on the hands
And she kissed their faces.
"Now that you are all here

I am happy that you have come,
And especially you, Almanzor,
Whom I have loved best of all.
To your horses once more, my sons,
And take your weapons with you,
For you must go and lodge
Out in Cantarranas.
In God's name, my sons, I beg you,
Do not go to the marketplace,
For the people are crowded together
And there are bitter quarrels."
Now the Princes have mounted,
Now they have gone to their lodgings;
They found the tables laid
And meat there in plenty;
After they had eaten
They sat down to play at tables.
That fair Doña Lambra,
Indulging her fantasy,
Had arrayed high targets
Along the riverbed.
One hurled the spear, then another,
But none struck the mark;
Then came a nobleman
From Bureba the costly,
A mounted knight
With a short spear in his hand.
He spurred forward

And flung his spear at the target,
Calling out: "Love, ladies,
Each one as you are beloved!
For there is more worth in one knight
From Bureba the costly
Than in seven or seventy
Sprung from the flower of Lara!"
Doña Lambra, when she heard him,
Was filled with delight:
"Oh cursed be the lady
Who would deny you her body!
Were it not that I am married
I would tender you my own!"
Doña Sancha has heard her
And in sorrow answers her:
"Be still, Lambra, be still,
You should not say such things,
For today you were promised in marriage
To Don Rodrigo de Lara."
"Be still yourself, Doña Sancha!
You would do well to say nothing,
Having brought forth seven sons
Like a sow in a quagmire!"
A knight who had reared the Princes
Overheard every word.
With tears streaming from his eyes,
In mortal rage and anguish,
He went out to the palace

Where the Princes were.
Some were playing at dice,
Some were playing at tables;
Gonzalo stood apart
Leaning against a railing:
"Tell me, what sorrow brings you,
My tutor, what has made you angry?"
Gonzalo insisted so long
That at last his teacher told him;
"Only, I beg you, my son,
Do not go to the marketplace."
Gonzalo would not have gone,
But his horse would not stay;
He galloped to the marketplace,
He asked for a spear,
He looked at the target
Which no one had yet struck down;
He stood up in the stirrups,
He brought it to the ground.
When he had struck it down
He spoke in this fashion:
"Love, love, shameless ladies,
Each one as you are beloved,
For there is more worth in one knight
Sprung from the flower of Lara
Than in forty or fifty
From Bureba the costly!"
Doña Lambra, when she heard it,

Stepped down in fury
And left the marketplace
Without waiting for her attendants,
And went to the palace
Where Don Rodrigo was,
And went in at the door
And gave tongue to her complaint:
"I have a grievance, Don Rodrigo!
I might as well be a widow!
I am ill-cherished in Castile
By those who should protect me!
The sons of Doña Sancha
Have insulted me to my face,
They have said that they would cut my skirts
In a shameful place,
And put a distaff in my belt
And make me spin,
And fatten their falcons
In my dovecote.
If you let this pass unavenged
I shall become a Mooress
And carry my complaint
To the good king Almanzor."
"Hush, hush, my lady,
Do not say such a thing,
I shall wreak full vengeance for you
Upon the Princes of Lara.
The web is in the frame,

It will soon be woven;
Men born and yet unborn
Will speak of it forever."

Second *Romance* of the Seven Princes of Lara

On the mountains of Altamira
Which are called the ridge of the Arabs
Don Rodrigo was waiting
For his sister's sons.
They were not slow in departing,
But the traitor grumbled and fretted
Swearing a great oath
On the cross of his sword
That he would sever the soul
From whoever detained the Princes.
It was their teacher who kept them,
Giving them good advice;
It was old Nuño Salido,
Who inspects the omens.
When he has counseled them all
He rides along with them;
Their mother accompanies them
For a full day's journey:
"Farewell, farewell, my sons,
May you come back to us soon!"
Now they ride away from their mother.
In the pine grove of Canicosa
They saw unpropitious omens,
Not to be made light of:
At the top of a dry pine tree
They saw a golden eaglet

Tormented to death
By a treacherous sparrowhawk.
Don Nuño saw the omen:
"We shall come to no good on this journey.
Seven forces of Moors
Are waiting for us in ambush.
In God's name I beg you, my lords,
Do not cross over the river,
For he who crosses over
Will never come back to Salas."

    In pure recklessness
Gonzalo answered him
(He was the youngest in days,
But a strong man in battle):
"Do not say so, my teacher,
For that is where we are going."
And he clapped spurs to his horse
And crossed over the river.

Third *Romance* of the Seven Princes of Lara

Now those seven brothers,
The same who are called the Princes,
Who are called the Princes of Lara,
Have fought until they are weary.
They cannot lift their arms,
So great is their weariness!
And Viara and Galve,
Almanzor's generals,
Are stricken with sorrow;
They curse the Princes' uncle
For leaving to their deaths
Noblemen of such valor,
Men who are sons, moreover,
Of his own sister.
They bring them away from the Moors,
Who do not wish to kill them.
They take them to their tents,
They take away their weapons,
They have sent for bread to give them,
And they have sent for drink.
Ruy Velazquez saw it
And said to Viara and Galve:
"An ill thing you are doing,
Allowing them to live,
For if they should escape
I shall not see Castile again,

For they will take my life,
I shall be helpless against them."
The Moors were filled with grief
When they heard what he said.
The youngest of the Princes
Spoke to him in anger:
"Oh false and fiendish traitor,
How vast is your perfidy!
You led us here with your host
To fight against the Moors,
The enemies of the faith,
And you have sold us to them,
And you urge them to kill us here.
May you get no pardon from God;
May He grant you no pardon ever
For today's heinous sin!"
The Moors answered the Princes,
This is what they said:
"We cannot decide how to treat you,
Oh Princes of great worth,
For if we should let you live,
Ruy Velazquez would go
To Almanzor, in Cordoba,
And he would become a Moor,
And they would give him great power,
And if he should send it against us
He would do us much injury,
For he is a man of great guile.

We will spare your lives and return you
To where the battle was;
Take arms and defend yourselves;
We are grieved at your ill fortune."
The Princes have armed themselves;
They have returned to the field.
Commending themselves to God
They await the Moors.
The Moors, at the sight of them,
With loud cries rode against them.
Then was a bloody battle!
How well they defended themselves!
The Moors were in such numbers
That they could not make way against them;
But they killed two thousand and seventy,
Not counting those whom they wounded.
Don Gonzalo, the youngest of all,
Was the one who wrought most carnage:
So many Moors he slaughtered!
So dearly he sold his life!
They are exhausted with fighting,
They can move no longer;
Their horses have been killed,
Their lances and swords are gone,
And all their other weapons
Have been broken in pieces.
The Moors have taken them captive.
They have stripped off their breastplates;

They have cut off their heads.
Ruy Velazquez beheld it all.
Don Gonzalo, the youngest of the seven,
Was overcome with anguish
At the sight of his dear brothers
Losing the heads from their shoulders;
He took heart again,
He broke from the arms that held him,
He set upon the Moor
Who was doing that butchery,
He struck him such a blow with his fist
That he left him dead on the ground.
He took up the man's sword.
He has killed twenty Moors.
They seized him again at last
And they cut off his head.
When all the Princes were dead
Ruy Velazquez turned away
Toward Burueva, his home.
He considered himself avenged,
Having arranged
This peerless treachery.

Fourth *Romance* of the Seven Princes of Lara

The *romance* is in the person of
Gonzalo Gustios, the Princes' father.

In sorrow I abide in Burgos,
Blind with weeping at my misfortunes,
Not knowing when the day rises
Nor when the night has come,
Were it not that with hard heart
Doña Lambra, who hates me,
Each day as the dawn breaks
Sends to wake my grief also:
So that I may weep for my sons
One by one, every day
She has her men throw
Seven stones at my window.

Doña Urraca Reminds the Cid of Their Youth in Zamora

"Away, away, Rodrigo,
Arrogant Castilian!
You should not have forgotten
The good days that are gone
When you were armed and knighted
At the altar of Santiago,
When the King was your godfather
And you, Rodrigo, his godchild;
Your arms my father gave you,
Your horse my mother gave you,
Your golden spurs I buckled on you
To your greater honor.
I thought we would be married;
For my sins it was not to be!
For you married Jimena,
Count Lozano's daughter;
Where she brought you money
I would have brought you kingdoms;
You turned from a king's daughter
To marry a vassal's child."
Rodrigo, at her words,
Was stung with anguish:
"Away, away, my vassals:
You knights and men-at-arms,

For I have been struck by an arrow
Shot from that strong tower;
With no iron on its shaft
It has gone through my heart;
And there is no cure for it,
I know, but sorrow!"

Romance of the Cid

> The Cid's vassals, mounting his body
> upon Babieca, defeat Búcar.

Dead lies that good Cid,
Rodrigo of Vivar.
Gil Díaz, his good servant,
Does as he was bidden.
He embalms the body;
He leaves it stiff and rigid;
Its face is beautiful,
Of great beauty and well colored,
Its two eyes equally open,
Its beard dressed with great care;
It does not appear to be dead,
But seems to be still alive,
And to make it stay upright
Gil Díaz proceeds with cunning:
He sets it in a saddle
With a board between its shoulders
And at its breast another;
At the sides these are joined together;
They go under the arms
And cover the back of the head.
So for the back, and another
Comes up as far as the beard,
Holding the body upright

So that it leans to no side.
Twelve days have passed
Since the death of the Cid.
His vassals armed themselves
To ride out to battle
Against that Moorish king Búcar
And the rabble he led.
When it was midnight
They placed upon Babieca
The body, prepared as it was,
And onto the horse they tied it.
It sits erect and upright,
It looks as though it were living,
With breeches on its legs
Embroidered black and white,
Resembling the hose he had worn
When he was alive.
They dressed it in garments
Adorned with needlework,
And his shield, at the neck,
Swung with its device.
A helmet on its head
Fashioned of painted parchment
Looks as though it were iron,
It was so well contrived.
In the right hand the sword Tizona
Was cunningly fastened;
It was wonderful to watch it

Go forward in the raised hand.
On one side rode the bishop,
The famous Don Jerome,
On the other Gil Díaz
Who guided Babieca.
Don Pedro Bermúdez rode forth
With the Cid's banner raised,
With four hundred nobles
In his company:
Then the main file advanced
With as many again for escort;
The Cid's corpse rode forth
With a brave company.
One hundred are the guardians
Who rode with the honored corpse,
Behind it goes Doña Jimena
With all her train,
With six hundred knights
There to be her guard:
They go in silence, so softly
You would say there were less than twenty.
Now they have left Valencia,
The clear day has dawned;
Alvar Fañez was the first
Who charged with fury
Upon the host of the Moors
Assembled with Búcar.
He found himself confronted

With a beautiful Mooress;
She was skilled at shooting
Arrows from a quiver
With a Turkish bow.
Star was what they called her
Because of her excellence
With the javelin.
She was the first who took horse
And rode forward
With a hundred others like her,
All valiant and daring.
The Cid's vassals charged them with fury
And left them dead on the ground.
King Búcar has seen them,
And the other kings who are with him.
They are filled with wonder
At the sight of the Christian host.
To them it looks as though
There are seventy thousand knights,
Each of them white as snow,
And one who fills them with dread,
Grown now more huge than ever,
Riding on a white horse,
A colored cross on his breast,
In his hand a white standard.
The sword looks like a flame
To spread carnage among the Moors;
Great slaughter it wields among them,

They flee, they do not wait.
King Búcar and the kings who are with him
Abandon the field;
They make straight for the sea
Where the ships were left.
The Cid's knights charge after them.
Not one of them escaped.
All gasped and sank in the sea;
More than ten thousand drowned.
All rushing there together,
Not one of them reached the ships.
Of the kings, twenty were killed.
Búcar escaped by flight.
The Cid's vassals seized the tents
And much gold and much silver.
The poorest was made rich
With what they took there.
They set out for Castile
As the good Cid had commanded.
They have come to San Pedro,
San Pedro of Cardeña.
There they have left his body
Whom all Spain has honored.

11. Single *Romances*

Rosaflorida

In Castile there is a castle
Called Rocafrida,
The castle is called Roca
And the fountain Frida.
Its walls are of fine silver,
Of gold its battlements,
And in each embrasure
There is a sapphire set
Which shines abroad at night
Like the sun at noon.
    Within there was a maiden
Named Rosaflorida;
She had seven counts for suitors,
Three dukes of Lombardy,
And she scorned them every one,
So lofty is her pride!
She fell in love with Montesinos,
From hearsay, not from sight;
And in her passion
She cried aloud at midnight.
She was heard by a chamberlain
Who was there as her tutor.
"What is this, my lady,
What is this Rosaflorida?
You must be tormented with love

Or else out of your senses!"
"Chamberlain, I bid you,
Carry my message.
Bear these letters for me
Into rich France.
Tell Montesinos,
Whom I most love,
To come to me
For Easter Sunday.
If he is unwilling
I will repay him.
I will clothe his squires
In scarlet apparel.
I will give him seven castles,
The finest in Castile.
Much more I will give him
If he desires more.
I will give him my body
Which has no peer for beauty
Unless it be for my sister's,
May bad fires consume her!
And if she is prettier
I am more fresh and graceful."

Count Arnaldos

Who ever will find such fortune
On the waters of the sea
As befell Count Arnaldos
On St. John's Day morning?
As he was going hunting
With his hawk on his hand
He saw a galley
Making in for the land.
Its sails were of silk,
Of fine silk its rigging,
The sailor at the helm
Came singing a song
At which the sea grew smooth
And the winds became gentle,
And the fish that go in the deep
Came swimming to the top,
And the birds that go flying
Came to perch on the mast.
Then spoke Count Arnaldos,
You will hear what he said:
"I beg you in God's name, sailor,
Repeat that song to me."
The sailor made him answer,

This was his reply:
"I repeat that song to no one
But to him who comes with me."

The Fair Princess

There was the fair princess
In the shade of an olive tree,
With a golden comb in her hands,
Combing and combing her hair.
She lifted her eyes toward heaven
On the side where the sun rises;
She saw a file of armed men
Coming up the Guadalquivir,
In its center Alfonso Ramos,
Admiral of Castile.
"Welcome, Alfonso Ramos,
Good fortune attend your arrival,
And from my bristling fleet
What news do you bring me?"
"I have tidings for you, my lady,
If you promise to spare my life."
"Speak out, Alfonso Ramos;
I promise that I will spare it."
"Yonder the Moors of Barbary
Are overrunning Castile."
"Had it not been for my promise
I would have seen your head fall."
"Were you to cut off my head
It would cost you your own."

Melisenda

If you know the pains of love,
In your grace, in your goodness,
Knight, if to France you go,
Ask for Gaiferos,
And tell him that his lady
Commends herself to him,
That his jousts and tourneys
Are famous among us,
And his courtliness
At praising the ladies.
Tell him for a certainty
That they will wed me:
Tomorrow I must marry
One from across the sea.

Death and the Lover

Last night I dreamed a dream,
A little dream, from my soul,
I dreamed about my love,
That I held her in my arms;
I saw a white lady enter,
White, whiter than the cold snow.
"Where did you come in, love?
How did you come in, my life?
The doors are closed, the windows,
The shutters."
"I am not love, young lover,
But Death, whom God has sent you."
"Ah Death, severe though you are,
One day of life grant me!"
"One day it cannot be,
One hour only."
In haste he put on his shoes,
In more haste his clothes,
And now he is in the street
Where his love lives.
"Open the door to me, white love,
Open the door to me, girl!"
"How should I open to you
When it is not time?
My father has not gone to the palace

Nor is my mother sleeping."
"Open to me this night
Or never, beloved;
Death is close behind me,
I would have life beside you."
"Go under the window
Where I stitched and embroidered,
I will throw you a silken cord
For you to climb;
If it does not reach to you
I will add my braided hair."
    The fine silk has broken
And on the instant Death was there:
"Let us depart, young lover,
For the hour is over."

Cool Fountain

Cool fountain, cool fountain,
Cool fountain where love is,
Where all the little birds
Go and find solace,
Except the turtledove
Who is widowed and full of sorrow.
Near that place there passed
The nightingale, that traitor:
"Lady, if it meets your pleasure,
It is mine to serve you."
"Away, be gone, tormentor,
Evil one, false one, deceiver,
For I perch neither on green bough
Nor in flowering meadow.
For if I find the water clear
Turbid I drank it,
For I desire no husband,
For I want no children, no,
Nor to take pleasure in them,
Nor any consolation.
Leave me, wretch, enemy,
Evil one, false one, foul traitor,
For I will not be your mistress
Nor marry you either, no!"

Fair Melisenda

Everyone was asleep
Who was in God's keeping,
But not Melisenda
The Emperor's daughter;
Love for Count Ayuelo
Would not let her rest.
She leapt out of bed
As her mother bore her,
She dressed herself in a smock,
For she could not find a shift,
She went through the palace
To where her ladies were;
Slapping them with her hand
She called out to them:
"If you are asleep, my maidens,
If you are asleep, come awake,
And you who know something of love
Be pleased to advise me,
And you who of love know nothing,
Keep this a secret for me.
Love for Count Ayuelo
Will not let me rest."
Then spoke an old woman,
Old, aged, and ancient:
"While you are a girl, daughter,

See to it that you have pleasure;
If you wait until you are old
Not a boy will desire you.
This I learned as a girl
(And I cannot forget it)
At the time when I was a servant
In your father's house."
When Melisenda had heard that
She waited to hear no more,
She went to find the Count
In the palace where he was,
She kept to the shadows of the eaves
So that no one should recognize her.
She met Hernandillo,
Her father's constable;
When he saw her walking alone
He began to cross himself:
"What is this, Melisenda,
What can this mean?
It must be that love torments you
Or else you are raving mad!"
"I am not tormented by love,
I pine for no one,
But once I had a sickness
When I was a child;
I promised to make a novena
There in St. John Lateran;
The ladies went in the daytime,

The maidens are going now."
When Hernando heard what she said
He answered nothing more;
But the enraged princess
Desired vengeance upon him:
"Now lend me, Hernando,
Lend me now your dagger,
For I am frightened, I am frightened
Of the dogs in the street."
By the point he took his dagger
And handed her the hilt;
Such a stroke she gave him
That he fell dead to the ground.
"Now go, Hernandillo,
And report to the King, my father."
And she went to the palace
Where Count Ayuelo was;
She found the doors locked,
And no way in;
With the art of enchantment
She flung open the doors.
Seven torches were burning there,
She put out every one.
The Count came awake
Filled with a great terror:
"Now God in heaven preserve me
And Santa María his mother!
Is it my enemies

Come to murder me,
Or is it my transgressions
Come to lead me astray?"
The cunning Melisenda
Began to speak to him:
"My lord, do not be alarmed,
Let fear have no place in you,
For I am a Moorish girl
Come from over the sea.
My body is as white
As a fine crystal;
My teeth are as tiny,
As tiny as salt,
My mouth is as red
As a fine coral."
Then spoke the good Count,
This answer he made her:
"I have made an oath,
I have sworn on a prayer book,
Never to deny my body
To any woman who should demand it,
Except Melisenda
The Emperor's daughter."
Then Melisenda
Fell to kissing him,
And in the black darkness
Their game is of Venus.

When the morning came
And it began to dawn,
He opened the shutters
In order to see the Mooress;
He saw that it was Melisenda
And he spoke to her:
"Lady, it would have been better
If you had killed me last night
Before so great an evil
Had been committed!"
He went to the Emperor
To tell him of this matter;
Kneeling upon the ground
He began to speak:
"I have brought you tidings
That are sorrowful to tell,
But see, here is the sword
With which to take vengeance on me;
For last night Melisenda
Came into my palace;
She told me that she was a Mooress
From over the sea,
And that she had come to sleep
And to have her pleasure with me.
And then, wretch that I am,
I let her lie beside me!"
Then spoke the Emperor
And made this reply:

"Put away, put away your sword,
For I wish you no injury;
But if you will have her, Count,
I will give her to you to marry."
Then the Count said: "I rejoice,
In my heart I am happy.
Whatever your Highness commands,
Here I am to obey."
They sent to fetch the bishop
To perform the ceremony;
They held rich celebrations
With great solemnity.

Tenderina

    Dukes and counts are going
Into the King's palace;
An old count entered there
With his son by the hand.
Tenderina has called him
Behind the main altar:
"God be my protection, boy,
If you were twenty-one
You should eat with me at table
And you should sleep beside me."
"If growth is all that counts, my lady,
I am as large as I need be."
"Silence, boy, silence, boy,
For you would boast about it."
"No woman ever gave me her body
And I boasted about it."
But the next day in the morning
He boasted about it:
"Such ease I had in my bed last night,
It was a dream of pleasure,
For I slept with Tenderina,
The Count of Saragossa's daughter."
"Silence, boy, silence, boy,
Oh ignorant boy;
If you have slept with a woman,

Her you shall marry."
"With this sword let them kill me,
With this sword at my side,
If ever I marry a woman
Who gave me her body."

When the Moon Was as High

When the moon was as high
As the sun at midday
The good German Count
Slept with the Queen,
And no one knew of it,
No one in the court,
Except the Princess,
Her own daughter.
In this manner
Her mother spoke to her:
"Princess, whatever you saw,
Whatever you saw keep secret;
The German Count will give you
A mantle of fine gold."
"A bad fire burn it, Mother,
That mantle of fine gold,
If I must have a stepfather
While my father is still living!"
Weeping, she went out from there
And met the King her father:
"Why are you crying, Princess?
Tell me, what made you weep?"
"I was sitting here at table
Eating bread soaked in wine,
And the German Count came in

And spilled it on my gown."
"Hush, daughter, hush, daughter,
Do not let it trouble you,
For the German Count is only a boy
And he did it jesting."
"Father, may a bad fire
Burn such laughter and jesting,
For he took me in his arms
And would have had his pleasure with me."
"If he took you in his arms
And would have had his pleasure with you,
Before the sun is in the sky
I shall send to take his life."

Knight, the Time Has Come

"Knight, the time has come,
It is time we went from here;
I cannot stand up to walk,
Nor wait on the Emperor;
For my belly is swollen,
My garments will not meet around me,
I am ashamed before my maidens
Who have to dress me,
They catch one another's eyes,
They never stop laughing;
I am ashamed before my knights
Who serve in my presence."
"I say give birth to it, lady,
As my mother did me;
For I am the son of a laborer
And a bread vendor bore me."
When the Princess heard what he said
She cursed and railed:
"Curses fall on any maid
Who would bear such a man's child!"
"Do not curse yourself, lady,
Do not call down curses;
My father is the King of France,
Doña Beatriz is my mother;
I have a hundred castles

In France, lady, to house you,
Kept by a hundred damsels,
Lady, to serve you."

Lanzarote

The King had three little sons,
Three little sons and no more,
And out of anger at them
He cursed them every one.
One turned into a stag,
Into a dog, another,
And the other turned into a Moor
And crossed the ocean waters.
Lanzarote was walking
At leisure among the ladies;
One of them cried out to him:
"Stay, knight, oh stay!
If such might be my fortune
My fate would be fulfilled
If I were to be married to you,
If it pleased you to wed me,
And if, for my bride-gift, you gave me
That stag with the white foot."
"With all my heart, my lady,
I would give it to you
If I knew the country
Where that stag was reared."
Now Lanzarote has taken horse,
Now he has mounted, and now he departs.
With him, ranging before him,

Are his two hounds on the leash.
He has come to a hermitage
Where a hermit is living:
"God watch over you, good man,
And a good welcome to you;
To judge from the hounds you have with you
It seems that you are a hunter."
"You that live in sanctity,
Hermit, tell me:
That stag with the white feet,
Where does he stay?"
"My son, do not go from this place
Before it is day;
I will tell you what I have seen
And all that is known to me.
This last night he went past here
Two hours before dawn;
Seven lions were with him
And a mother lioness.
Seven counts are lying dead,
And of knights a great number.
God preserve you forever, my son,
Wherever you go,
For whoever sent you to this place
Hoped never again to see you.
Ah, Lady Quintañones,

May a bad fire burn you,
Since so many excellent knights
Have lost their lives for you!"

The Mistress of Bernal Francés

I am all alone in my bed
Making love to my pillow;
Who could he be, this knight
Who at my door calls, "Open"?
"I am Bernal Francés, lady,
Who for some time have served you,
In your bed in the nighttime
And by day in your garden."
       She lifted back the Holland sheets,
She wrapped a shawl around her,
She took a golden candlestick
And went down to open the door.
No sooner was the door ajar
Than he blew out the candle.
"Our Lady keep me in her care,
And my lord Saint Giles protect me,
For He who has put out my candle
Could put out my life as easily!"
"Do not be frightened, Catalina;
I want no one to see me,
For I have killed a man in the street
And justice follows close behind me."
She has taken him by the hand
And led him to her chamber,
And made him sit in a silver chair

With a back of ivory,
And she has bathed his whole body
With Balm Gentle water,
She has made him a bed of roses
And a bolster of gilliflowers.
"What is troubling you, Bernal Francés,
That you are sad as you lie there?
Are you afraid of justice?
The watch will not enter here.
Are you afraid because of my servants?
They are sound asleep."
"I am not afraid of justice,
For I seek it for myself,
Still less do I fear the servants,
Sleeping their sound sleep."
"What is troubling you, Bernal Francés?
You were never so before.
You have left another love in France,
Or someone has spoken ill of me."
"I have left no other love in France,
For I never served another."
"If you are afraid because of my husband,
He is far, far away from here."
"Far, far away can become near
If a man wants to travel,
And as for your husband, my lady,
He is lying here beside you.
As a present upon my homecoming

I shall dress you in rich apparel:
I shall dress you in fine scarlet
With a red lining,
And such a crimson necklace
As I never saw on a lady;
I shall give you my sword for a necklace
To go around your neck.
And word will go to your Francés
That he can mourn for you."

The Fair Maid

"You are more fair, my lady,
Than a ray of the sun;
Can I sleep this night
Disarmed and without fear?
For it has been seven years, seven,
Since I took off my armor;
My flesh is blacker
Than a sooty coal."
"You can sleep this night, sir,
Disarmed and without fear,
For the Count has gone hunting
To the mountains of León."
"May his dogs die of rabies,
Eagles strike his falcons,
And his chestnut steed drag him
Home from the mountain."
While they were talking
Up rode her husband.
"What are you doing, fair daughter
Of a treacherous father?"
"I am combing my hair, my lord,
And in great sorrow
Because you left me alone
And went to the mountains."
"Your answer, maid,

Was false from beginning to end.
Whose is that horse
That neighed below there?"
"It comes from my father, my lord,
And he sent it for you."
"Whose are those weapons
In the gallery?"
"They come from my brother, my lord,
He sent them today."
"Whose is that lance
That I can see from here?"
"Take it, Count, take it,
And kill me with it,
For such a death I merit,
Good Count, at your hands."

The Enchanted Princess

The knight has gone hunting, hunting,
As often before,
His hounds are weary,
He has lost his falcon.
Against an oak he leaned,
It was marvelously high;
On a branch at the top
He saw a little princess;
The hair of her head
Covered all of that oak tree.
"Knight, do not be afraid,
Nor draw back with dread,
For I am the good King's daughter,
My mother is Queen of Castile.
Seven fairies bewitched me
In my nurse's arms
To remain for seven years
Alone on this mountain.
It is seven years today,
Or at dawn tomorrow.
Knight, in God's name I beg you,
Take me away with you,
To be your wife if you please,
Or if not, your mistress."
"Wait for me, my lady,

Until dawn tomorrow.
I will go to my mother nearby
And ask her to advise me."
The girl gave him an answer,
These are the words she spoke:
"Oh knight, you are wrong and foolish
To leave me here alone!"
But he goes to get advice
And leaves her on the mountain.
The advice that his mother gave him
Was to take her for his mistress.
When the knight returned to the place
He could not find the princess.
He saw a great procession
Bearing her away.
The knight, when he beheld it,
Fell down onto the ground,
And when he came to his senses
The words he spoke were these:
"The knight who could lose such a thing
Deserves a heavy penance:
I will be my own judge,
I will pronounce my own sentence:
Let them cut off my feet and hands
And through the town drag me."

Fresh Rose

"Fresh rose, fresh rose,
Most fair and loving,
When I had you in my arms
I did not know how to serve you,
And now when I would have you
I cannot serve you, no."
"You are to blame for that, friend,
You, and not me, no.
You sent a letter to me
Through a servant of yours
Who never gave it to me
But told me a different story:
He said you were married, friend,
There in the lands of León,
And had a wife of great beauty
And children like a flower."
"Whoever told you that, lady,
Did not tell you the truth, no,
For I never set foot in Castile,
Nor there in the lands of León,
Except when I was little
And knew nothing of love."

Constancy

My ornaments are arms,
My repose is fighting,
My bed the hard stones,
My sleep endless watching;
The houses are dark,
The roads yet to travel,
Heaven with its changes
Delights to do me evil;
Going from crag to crag
By the shores of the ocean,
Seeking whether any place
Might ease my fortune.
But for you, my lady,
All must be borne.

The Prisoner

It was May, the month of May,
When warm days are with us,
When the grain gets its growth
And the fields are in flower,
When the skylark sings
And the nightingale gives answer,
When those who are in love
Go in love's service,
Except for me, wretch, living
In sorrow in this prison,
Not knowing when it is day
Nor when night has come
Except for a little bird
Which sang to me at dawn;
A man killed it with a crossbow,
God give him an ill reward!

One Castle, Two Castles

There was a princess who held
One castle, two castles,
And there were twelve counts
Who all wanted to marry her,
And there was a squire of hers
Who waited upon her.
She said: "Squire, good squire,
You would do me great kindness
If you were to take this letter
To the knight of Encina,
And if he would come to see me
I would reward his journey
With garments worked with gold,
All worked with gold and fine silver;
If this should not content him
Another thing I would give him.
I would give him two castles
That look out on the sea,
And in the keep of each castle
A hundred men-at-arms,
With their wages in order
For a year and a day.
If he is still unsatisfied
I will give him myself besides."

The Corpse-keeper

Seven years I have kept him, dead
And hidden in my chamber.
I change the shirt on him
Every holiday of the year.
I have anointed his face
With roses and white wine.
I have watched his bones laid bare
Of their white white flesh.
Alas, what can I do,
Wretch, in my disgrace?
Should I tell my father
He would say it is my lover;
Should I tell my mother
I would have no peace after;
Should I tell my sister
She knows nothing of love;
Should I tell my brother
He is the man to kill me;
Should I tell the constable
He would have me punished.
Better for me to say nothing,
To endure it and hold my tongue.
One day at my balcony,
Looking from my window,
I saw a huntsman passing

Who hunts in our crags.
"Huntsman, good huntsman,
One word, hear me:
Will you bury a dead body?
You will be rewarded.
And not in worthless coppers
But in gold and silver."
Going down the stairs
Two thousand kisses I gave him:
"Farewell, delight of my life,
Farewell, delight of my soul;
It will not be long
Before I come and visit you."

Knight, Where Are You Going

"Knight, where are you going,
Leaving me alone?
I have three little children
Who cry and call for bread."
"I have left you fields and vineyards
And half of a city."
"That will not suffice me
Nor provide me with bread."
He put his hand into his breast
And gave her a hundred doubloons:
"If in seven years I am still gone,
In the eighth year you must marry."
His mother heard what he said
And she muttered a curse.
Time came and time went.
Remorse overcame her.
She went and stood at the window
That looked out on the ocean,
And she saw galleons
On the sea sailing.
"Have you set eyes on my son,
The child of my body?"
"I have seen your son,
The child of your body.
He had a stone for his pillow

And sand for his coverlet,
There were three knife-wounds in him,
The sun entered through one
And the moon through another;
In and out of the smallest
A sparrow-hawk was flying."
His mother when she heard it
Would have leapt down into the sea.
"Do not throw yourself down, Mother,
For I am your own son."
"If you are my own son
What proof can you give me?"
"That little moon-shaped mark
Under your left breast."
They clasped hand in hand
And fled away together.

Upon These Seas

Upon these seas sailing
As fortune bore me
I came to foreign lands
Where none knew me,
Where no cockerel crowed
Nor hen called aloud,
Where the orange grows,
The lemon, the citron,
And a vase of rue stands guard
Over the creature.
Ah Julián, false betrayer,
Author of my troubles,
You came into my gardens
And you deceived me!
Ah, you picked my flower,
You plucked it grain by grain!
Ah, with your delicate talk
And you deceived me!
Ah, and highborn as I was
They married me to Julián,
The gardener's son
From my own garden.
Ah Julián, let us go

From this unkind place;
Let rain fall down from heaven
Upon us.

There Was a Beautiful Lady

There was a beautiful lady,
No one was more lovely:
She wore frock upon frock,
A sumptuous skirt,
A blouse of Holland linen,
A tunic and collar of pearls.
Her forehead is dazzling,
And her hair is of brass,
Her brow mother-of-pearl,
Her eyes almonds,
Her nose fine as a feather,
Her cheeks roses,
Her mouth very rounded,
Her teeth pearls,
Slender her throat,
Pomegranates her breasts,
Her waist small, her body
Drawn fine like a cyprus.
When she went in to hear Mass
The church danced with light.
There the musician saw her
As he played on an instrument.
"Play on, play on, wretch."
As she kneeled down she said:
"For I have come for you,

Because the one I came for
Is not at Mass, no.
Seven years I have waited for him
As an honorable woman.
After eight years without him
In the ninth I will marry.
Let the King of France take me,
Or the Duke of Stambul.
If the Duke will not have me
The musician can take me;
Let him play to me day and night
And sing to me at dawn."
They clasped hand in hand
And went away together.

Face Like a Flower

"Open the door to me,
Open it, face like a flower;
You have been mine since you were a child,
How much more so now."
She with the face like a flower
Went down and opened the door;
They went to the garden
Hand in hand together.
Under a green rose tree
They set their table.
Eating and drinking
They fell asleep together.
When it was midnight
He awoke lamenting:
"What pain I have in my side,
Here in my side!"
"I will bring a learned doctor
For your healing,
I will give you a bag of money
For your spending,
I will bring you fresh bread
For your eating."
"When you have killed a man
You talk of healing!"

The Invitation

"Mariana, I am invited
To a wedding on Sunday."
"That wedding, Don Alonso,
Should be between you and me."
"It is not my wedding, Mariana,
The groom is a brother of mine."
"Sit down here, Don Alonso,
On this flowered bench
Which was left to me by my father
For the man who should marry me."
Don Alonso sat down there
And soon he was asleep.
Mariana, in silence,
Crept out to the flowering garden.
Three ounces of corrosive,
Four of powdered steel,
The blood of three serpents,
A live lizard's skin
And the shinbone of a toad
She put into the wine.
"Drink some wine, Don Alonso;
Don Alonso, drink some wine."
"After you, Mariana,
For that's as it should be."
Sly Mariana

Poured it down her dress.
Don Alonso, like a young man,
Drank it at one draught.
So strong was the poison
That his teeth fell out of his head.
"What is this, Mariana?
What is this in the wine?"
"Three ounces of corrosive,
Four of powdered steel,
The blood of three serpents,
A live lizard's skin
And the shinbone of a toad
To deprive you of your life."
"Good Mariana, cure me
And I will marry you."
"Don Alonso, it cannot be
For your heart is cleft in two."
"Farewell, bride of my soul,
Soon you will have no husband.
Farewell, Father and Mother,
Soon you will have no son.
When I left my house
On a piebald horse I rode,
And now I shall go to the church
In a box of pinewood."

King Ramiro and His Commanders

Now King Ramiro is seated,
Now he has sat down to dine;
Three of his commanders
Have appeared before him.
One is named Armiño,
Another is named Galvane,
And a third is Tello, wearing
The star of a commander.
"May God preserve you, my lord."
"Commanders, you are welcome.
What tidings do you bring me
From the field of Palomares?"
"We bring you good news, my lord,
As we come from that place.
We journeyed seven days
And never ate bread,
Nor were the horses fed,
Which grieved us worse,
And we found no inhabited place
Nor a soul to speak to
Except for seven huntsmen
Who had gone hunting there,
And whether we would or no
We had to fight with them.
Four of them we killed,

Three we brought back with us.
Good King, if you do not believe us
They themselves will bear witness."

The Gray She-wolf

As I was in my hut
Painting my shepherd's crook
The Pleiades were climbing
And the moon waning;
Sheep are poor prophets
Not to keep to the fold.
I saw seven wolves
Come up through a dark gully.
They cast lots as they came
To see who should enter the fold;
It fell to an old she-wolf,
Gray, grizzled, and bowlegged,
With fangs lifting her lips
Like the points of knives.
Three times she circled the fold
And could take nothing;
Once more she went round it
And snatched the white lamb,
The Merino's daughter,
Niece of the earless ewe,
Which my masters were saving
For Easter Sunday.
"Come here, my seven pups,
Here, my bitch from Trujilla,
Here, you on the chain,

Run down the gray she-wolf.
If you fetch back the lamb
On milk and bread you will dine;
Fail to fetch her back,
You'll dine on my stick."
On the heels of the she-wolf
They wore their nails down to crumbs;
Seven leagues they ran her
On the harsh mountains.
Climbing a little ravine,
The she-wolf begins to tire:
"Here, dogs, you can take the lamb,
As sound and well as ever."
"We do not want the lamb
From your wolving mouth;
Your skin is what we want,
For a coat for the shepherd,
Your tail to make laces
To fasten his breeches,
Your head for a bag
To keep spoons in,
And your guts for lute strings
To make the ladies dance."

The Hill Girl

Mother, as I was going
To Villa Real
I lost my way
In a rough place.
Seven days I went on
And I ate no bread,
Nor my mule barley,
Nor my falcon meat.
Between Zarzuela
And Durazután
I raised my eyes
To the side where the sun rises;
I saw a little house
And smoke rising from it.
I spurred my mule
And traveled toward it.
Sheep dogs came out
To bark at my heels.
I saw a hill girl
Of exquisite grace:
"Come in, come in, sir,
Do not be shy,
My father and mother
Have gone to the village,
My lover Minguillo

Has gone for bread
And will not be back
Till tomorrow at supper;
You can drink milk
While the cheese is making.
We will make our bed
In the broom together.
We will make a boy baby,
We will call him Pascual,
He will be an archbishop,
Pope, cardinal,
Or else a swineherd
In Villa Real.
In good faith, my joy,
You should be merry."

Up There on the Mountain

Up there on the mountain
There goes a shepherd weeping;
So many tears have spilled from his eyes
That his coat is drenched with them.
Do not bury me in holy ground
If I die of this pain,
Bury me out in the meadow
Where no flocks go past.
Let my hair lie outside the grave,
Carefully combed and curled,
So that those who pass by may say:
"Here he died in misery."
There were three ladies who passed there,
All three of them weeping.
One of them said: "Farewell, my cousin!"
The next: "Farewell, my brother!"
But she who was the youngest
Said: "Farewell, my true love!"

Catalina

I went soft about a girl
In my heart and soul,
They called her Catalina,
I can't forget her, no.
She pled with me to take her
To the lands of Aragon.
"You're still a girl, Catalina,
You can't travel, no."
"I'll go as far, as far, sir,
And afoot, as you will go.
If money's what dissuades you
I'll bring enough for two,
Ducats for Castile
And florins for Aragon."
And the constables surprised them
As they were talking so.

The Cock and the Vixen

"Vixen you're out early
In this nasty weather."
"No, friend, none too early
When you think what I'm out for.
In my right cheek here
I've a tooth that's killing me.
If you would pull it for me
I'd do you some other favor."
"Close your eyes, then, vixen."
And the cock flew onto the roof-tree.
"Cock-a-doodle come down, come down!
Come down, cock crow!"
"The first time that you caught me
You pulled out all my tail,
And the next time you won't leave me
With a whole bone in my body!"

My Mother Made Me Marry

My mother made me marry,
When I was pretty and little,
A rogue, a boy,
Whom I didn't love at all.
When it struck midnight
Out went the rogue,
Cloak on shoulder
And his sword slung on.
I followed his footsteps
To see where he would go,
And I saw him enter
His lady-love's house.
I went close to listen
To hear what he would say
And I heard him tell her:
"For you, my little dove,
I intend to purchase
Petticoats and shawls,
And I'll give that other woman
A stick and bad times."
I went back home
In sorrow and dismay.
I sat down to eat
But eat I could not,
I sat down to sew

But sew I could not,
I got down to pray
But pray I could not.
I went to the balcony
To see if he was coming.
I heard his footsteps
Coming up the street.
He came to the door
And he called out and said:
"Open to me, open to me,
Open the door, love,
For I've come home weary
From making us a living."
"You've come home, liar,
From your lady-love,
I distinctly heard you tell her:
'For you, my little dove,
I intend to purchase
Petticoats and shawls,
And I'll give that other woman
A stick and bad times.'"

The Garland

"Daughter, that garland of roses,
Who gave it to you?"
"It was given me by a knight
Who went past my door;
He came and took me by the hand
And led me to his house;
There in a dark little doorway
He had his pleasure with me.
He laid me on a bed of roses
Where I had never lain before;
What he did to me I cannot say,
But what he did I loved him for.
Mother, I have got my shift
Stained with blood all over."
"Oh terrible catastrophe!
Oh, my wits are reeling!
If what you say is true, daughter,
Your honor is not worth a thing,
For people talk maliciously
And goodbye to your reputation."
"Mother, Mother, say no more,
My dear mother, be still;
Better a good lover
Than to be married and married ill.
For my part give me a good lover,

A good cloak and petticoat, Mother,
For she is a miserable creature
Who has a bad husband to cover her."
"If that is as you prefer it, daughter,
If that is your pleasure, I want no better."

Mathathias Weeping at the Destruction of Jerusalem

"Alas!" said the good father
To his five sons,
"Why should I have survived
To behold this day?
In my soul's sorrow to see
The holy city
In the hands of the enemy
Who slaughter without mercy
Old people and children
And plunder wherever they can,
And enforce sacrifice
To their idolatry."
In his grief he rose up
As though to worship
And by his own hand perished
On the altar where he lay.

Don García

Don García is walking
Along the top of a wall,
With arrows of gold in one hand
And a bow in the other.
He calls down curses on Fortune,
He recounts her abuses:
"When I was a child the King reared me,
God was a cloak around me;
A horse and arms he gave me
Excelling all others;
He gave me Doña María
To be my wife and consort,
He gave me a hundred maidens
To wait upon her,
He gave me the Castle of Uraña
As her dowry,
He gave me a hundred knights
To keep the castle,
He provided me with wine,
He provided me with bread,
He provided me with sweet water,
For there was none in the place.
The Moors laid siege to me there
On St. John's Day in the morning.
Seven years have come and gone

And the siege has not been lifted.
I have seen my people die
Because I had nothing to give them.
I set them up on the ramparts
With their weapons in their hands
So that the Moors should think
That they were ready for battle.
In the Castle of Uraña
There is only one loaf of bread.
If I give it to my children
What then of my wife?
If I were so base as to eat it
They would not forgive me."
He broke the bread into four pieces
And flung it down into the camp.
One of the four pieces
Rolled to the King's feet:
"Allah, here is grief for my Moors!
Allah is pleased to afflict them.
From his castle's overabundance
He supplies our encampment!"
And he bade them sound the trumpets
And they lifted their siege.

Romances of Valdovinos

I

The moon is as high
As the sun at noon
As Valdovinos comes forth
From the aqueduct of Seville.
There he happened to meet
A pretty Moorish girl;
Seven years Valdovinos
Had her for his mistress.
At the end of seven years
Valdovinos heaved a sigh.
"Did you sigh, Valdovinos,
My love, whom I most love?
It must be that you fear the Moors
Or love another mistress."
"Neither do I fear the Moors
Nor still less love another mistress,
But with you Moorish and I a Christian,
We lead a life of wickedness:
It is like eating meat on Friday,
My law forbids it."
"For love of you, Valdovinos,
I will become a Christian,
To be your wife, if you choose,
Or if not, your mistress."

Through the aqueduct of Carmona
Where the water flows to Seville,
There went Valdovinos
And his pretty mistress,
Feet in the water,
One hand on his armor,
For fear of the Moors,
Lest they should be spied.
Mouth to mouth they joined,
With none to forbid them;
In dismay Valdovinos
Heaved a sigh.
"Why do you sigh, my lord,
My heart and my life?
It must be that you fear the Moors
Or have a mistress in France."
"Neither do I fear the Moors
Nor have I a mistress in France,
But with you Moorish and I a Christian
We lead a most wicked life:
We eat meat on Friday,
Which my law forbids.
It is seven years, seven,
Since last I heard Mass.
If the Emperor knew of it
It would cost me my life."
"For love of you, Valdovinos,

I would become a Christian."
"And I, lady, for you,
A Moor among Moors."

III. Historical *Romances*

The Siege of Baza

The King was beside Baza
Monday, after he had dined;
He looked at the proud tents
Of the army's encampment;
He looked at the spreading fields
And the outlying hamlets;
He looked at the heavy parapet
Girdling the city;
He looked at the thick towers,
Too many to be counted.
A Moor behind a battlement
Called out to him:
"Go somewhere else, King Fernando,
Do not spend the winter here,
For the weather of this country
Will be more than you can bear.
We have bread enough for ten years,
A thousand beeves for salting,
We have twenty thousand Moors here
All capable of fighting;
We have eight hundred horsemen
To ride out skirmishing;
We have seven nobles

Each one as valiant as Roland,
And each of them has sworn
To die rather than yield."

Romances of the Siege of Baeza

I

Moors, my young Moors,
You that win my sustenance,
Break down Baeza for me,
That towered city;
And its old men and old women,
Put them all to the sword,
And its young boys and young girls,
Let the riders carry them off,
And Pedro Díaz's daughter
To be my beloved,
And her sister Leonor
To keep her company.
Go, Captain Vanegas,
The greater honor be yours,
For if I send you
I am sure of your return,
And that you will not suffer
Indignity or outrage.

II

That Moor Andalla Mir
Has laid siege to Baeza.
Eighty thousand foot
And ten thousand knights are with him,

And with him is that traitor,
That traitor Pedro Gil.
At the Gate of Bedmar
They begin the fighting;
They set ladders to the wall,
They begin to prevail,
They have taken one tower,
No one can resist them.
Then from the tower of Calonge
I saw fighters come out.
Ruy Fernandez goes in front,
That intrepid chief;
He attacks Andalla,
He closes in to strike him,
He has cut off his head;
The rest take to flight.

The Ancient and True *Romance* of the Siege of Alora

Alora, the well surrounded,
You that are by the river,
The Governor went to besiege you
On a Sunday morning.
With foot soldiers and men-at-arms
The field was well furnished;
With the great artillery
He has made a breach in your wall.
You would have seen Moors and their women
Fleeing into the castle,
The women carrying clothing
And the men flour and wheat,
And the Moorish girls of fifteen
Carrying fine gold,
And the little Moorish boys
Carrying figs and raisins.
They had flown their banner
From the peak of the wall.
There was a young Moor posted
Behind a battlement
With a bolt ready in his crossbow
And his crossbow drawn.
He called with a loud voice
So that the people heard him:

"A truce, Governor, a truce!
The castle surrenders to you!"
The Governor lifts his visor
To see who had addressed him.
The bolt was aimed at his forehead,
It came out through the back of his skull.
Pablo led his horse by the reins,
Little James took his hand,
Those two whom he had reared from children
In his own household.
They took him to the surgeons
To see whether they could heal him.
The first words he uttered
Were his will and testament.

The King of Aragon

The King of Aragon looked out
One day from Campo-Viejo,
He looked out on the Spanish sea
Where the tides fall and rise,
He looked at the ships and galleys
Departing and arriving,
Some were vessels from the fleet,
Others merchantmen,
Some take the route for Flanders,
Others for Lombardy,
Those that come from the war,
How gallant their appearance!
He gazed upon the great city,
Naples is its name,
He looked at the three castles
Of that great city,
Castelnuovo, Capuana,
And Santelmo, shining,
Shining out among them
Like the sun at noon.
He wept from his eyes
And he said: "Oh city
How dear you have cost me,
To my great sorrow!
You have cost me counts and dukes,

Men of great worth,
You have cost me a brother
Dear as a son to me,
And of the others, the common soldiers,
Beyond count or comparison.
Twenty-two years you have cost me,
The best years I shall see,
For in you my beard darkened upon me
And in you it has turned gray."

IV. Moorish *Romances* and *Romances* of Captives

Julianesa

"Move on, dogs, move on!
May you die of the rabies!
Thursday you kill the hog
And you eat his flesh on Friday.
Alas, seven years today
I have walked this valley,
Whence my unshod feet,
My nails running blood,
The raw flesh that I eat
And red blood I drink,
In sorrow seeking Julianesa,
The Emperor's daughter,
Whom the Moors stole from me
On St. John's Day morning, early,
Picking roses and flowers
In an orchard of her father's."
Julianesa has heard him,
In the Moor's arms where she lies;
The tears from her eyes
Down the Moor's face fall.

Reduán

"I am certain that you must remember,
Reduán, the promise you made me
To take the city of Jaén
In one night and give it to me.
Reduán, be as good as your word
And I shall double your pay,
But should you fail to do it
I will banish you from Granada
And send you to the frontier
Where you cannot enjoy your lady."
    With unmoved countenance
Reduán answered: "If ever
I said it I have forgotten,
But I will keep my promise."
    He asked for a thousand men,
The king gave him five thousand.
A great cavalcade rode out
There through the Gate of Elvira:
So many Moorish nobles,
So many bay mares,
So many gripped lances,
So many white bucklers,
So many green robes,
So many scarlet coats,
Such feathers and pageantry,

So many crimson cloaks,
So many fawn buskins,
So many handsome bowknots,
So many golden spurs,
So many stirrups of silver!
All of them valiant fighters
And veterans in battle,
And in the midst of them rode
The Boy King of Granada.
    The Moorish ladies were watching
From the towers of the Alhambra.
His mother, the Queen of the Moors,
Spoke to him in this manner:
"Allah preserve you, my son,
Mohammed be with you and keep you
And bring you back from Jaén
Free, unharmed, and in triumph,
And send you peace with your uncle
The lord of Guadix and Baza."

Fragment of a *Romance*

It was on the Eve of the Kings...

It was on the Eve of the Kings,
The first holy day of the year,
When the son of the Moorish King
Begged a boon of his father.
I ask for no gold, no silver,
No luxury,
But for twenty thousand men
To ride out behind me.
Let no goats be left, no sheep,
No shepherd with his flock...

Altamare

The King of the Moors had a son,
They called him Taquino:
He fell in love with Altamare,
His own dear sister.
When he saw that it could not be
He took to his sickbed.
There his father paid him a visit
On a Monday morning.
"What ails you, son Taquino,
What ails you, child of my soul?"
"Father, it is a fever
Which has pierced my soul."
"Shall I roast a bull for you,
One that we have reared ourselves?"
"Father, roast a bull for me
But let my sister serve it to me,
And let her when she comes to me
Come by herself with no company."
And as it was in summer
She was wearing white petticoats.
As soon as she came in at the door
Like a lion he bore down on her
And he seized her by the hand
And back upon the bed he forced her
And took his joy of that fair lily

And that freshly budded rose.
"Let punishment descend from heaven
Since there is none on earth!
Upon my father let it fall
For he has been the cause of it all."

The Moorish King Who Lost Granada

The Moorish King was riding
Through the city of Granada,
From the Gate of Elvira
To the Gate of Vivarrambla,
Alas for my Alhama!
Letters had come to him to say
That Alhama had been taken;
He threw the letters into the fire
And killed the messenger.
Alas for my Alhama!
He got down from the mule he was riding
And he mounted a horse;
Up to the Zacatín
He rode to the Alhambra.
Alas for my Alhama!
When he came into the Alhambra
He commanded them
To blow upon their trumpets,
Their long horns of silver.
Alas for my Alhama!
And to beat upon the war drums
A quick call-to-arms
So that his Moors should hear it
In Vega and Granada.
Alas for my Alhama!

All the Moors who heard the sound
Which summons to bloody Mars
One by one and two by two
Formed up in a great array.

Alas for my Alhama!

Then spoke a venerable Moor,
He spoke in this manner:
"King, why have you sent for us?
What is this summons for?"

Alas for my Alhama!

"You must be acquainted, my friends,
With a new calamity:
Christians of great bravery
Have taken from us Alhama."

Alas for my Alhama!

There spoke an elder
With a long beard and gray hair:
"That's just as you deserve, good King,
Good King, that's what you deserve!

Alas for my Alhama!

You killed the Abencerrajes,
The flower of Granada;
You laid hands on the renegades
From renowned Cordoba.

Alas for my Alhama!

For what you have done, King, you deserve
The heaviest penalty:

You deserve to lose your life and kingdom
And here to lose Granada!"

Alas for my Alhama!

Governor of the Moors

"Governor of the Moors,
You with the fine beard,
The King has sent to seize you
For the loss of Alhama."
"If the King has sent to seize me
For the loss of Alhama
The King will have his way,
But I owe him nothing.
For I had gone to Ronda
To my cousin's wedding
And had left behind in Alhama
The best guard I could muster.
If the King lost his city
I lost everything that I had;
I lost my wife and children,
The things which I most loved."

The Mooress Morayma

I was the Mooress Morayma,
A Moorish girl, and pretty;
A Christian came to my door,
Alas for me, to deceive me.
In Moorish speech he addressed me,
And he knew it well:
"Open the door to me, Moorish girl,
Allah keep you from evil."
"Open to you, oh wretch that I am,
Not knowing who you may be?"
"I am the Moor Mazote,
Your own mother's brother;
I have killed a Christian,
The constable is close behind me;
Unless you let me in, my life,
You will see them kill me here."
Alas for me, when I heard this
I rose up from my bed,
I threw a little cloak around me,
Not finding my silk shift;
I went over to the door
And I opened it all the way.

Then the Two Kings Sat Down

Then the two kings sat down
And the white Moor made three
And the white girl with them.
Then they sat down to play,
To play their game of chess.
One plays, the other plays,
They play all three.
Then the white Moor wins,
He wins once, he wins twice,
He wins three times.
"Why are you weeping, white girl?
Why are you weeping, white flower?
If you are weeping for your father
He is my jailer,
If you are weeping for your mother
She is my cook,
If you are weeping for your brothers
I have killed them all three."
"I am not weeping for my father, my mother,
Nor for my three brothers.
I am weeping only
For my own fortune."
"Your fortune, my lady,
Is here at your side."
"If you are my fortune, give me

That little knife of cyprus wood.
I will send it to my mother
So that she can rejoice at my fortune."
Hilt first the white Moor gave it to her.
The white girl took it, turned it,
And buried it in her breast.

My Father Was from Ronda

My father was from Ronda,
My mother from Antequera;
The Moors took me prisoner
Between peace and war,
And they bore me off to sell me
At Jerez de la Frontera.
Seven days and their nights
I was there at auction;
Not a Moorish man nor woman
Would give money for me
Except for one dog of a Moor
Who gave a hundred gold pieces,
And to his house took me
And snapped a chain on me
And he gave me a foul life,
A black life he led me:
Pounding hemp by day,
By night milling fodder
With a bit in my mouth
Lest I should eat any,
And my hair in a knot,
And I went round on a chain.
But as pleased God in heaven
He had a kind housekeeper:
When the Moor went hunting,

From the chain she released me
And in her lap took me
And picked the lice from my head;
For a favor that I did her
One far greater she did me:
She gave me the hundred gold pieces
And sent me back to my country,
And thus it pleased God in heaven
That I came to safety.

The Three Captive Girls

By the green, green,
By the green olive,
There my three girls
Were taken captive.
The sly Moor
Who captured them
To the Queen of the Moors
Delivered them.
"What are the names
Of these three captives?"
"The eldest Constanza,
The next Lucia,
And the youngest of all
They call Rosalia."
"What tasks shall we give
To these three captives?"
"Constanza to knead,
To sift, Lucia,
And the youngest of all
To fetch them water."
One day, fetching water
From the cold fountain,
She met an old man
Who was drinking there.
"Good old man, what brings you

To the cold fountain?"
"I am waiting to see
My three captive daughters."
"Then you are my father
And I am your daughter.
I must go and tell
My little sisters."
"Let me tell you, Constanza,
I must tell you, Lucia,
How I met Father
At the cold fountain."
Constanza wept
And Lucia sighed
But the youngest of all,
Hear what she said:
"Do not cry, Constanza,
Do not sigh, Lucia,
For the Moor, when he comes,
Will give us our freedom."
The sly Moorish woman
Who overheard them
Opened the dungeon
And put them in.
The Moor, when he came,
Let them out again,
And to their poor father
Delivered them.

Epitaph of Albayaldos Sarracino

This trophy hanging
From the branch of this pine tree
Was Albayaldos Sarracino's
Who had no peer for bravery
Among the Moors of Granada.
Could Alexander make his way
To this sepulcher, he would weep,
Stung with more anguish and envy
Than when he wept at the grave of that Greek
Whom great Homer had sung.

v. Late Lyric *Romances*

Fragment of a *Romance*

    I must tell you how it was with me
When I was in love:
My nights were misery,
Worse were my days,
In my mistress's service,
To win her sympathy.

That Shepherdess, Mother

That shepherdess, Mother,
With the blue eyes,
Ah God, she consumes my soul
Which is snow, and her eyes are fire!
When I make bold to adore her,
Well content with a poor reward,
She is a sea to my will
And a cliff to my desires.
But at the sight of those mountains,
Since my grief is assured,
Humbly and not in pride
I try to make myself heard;
But seeing that she is stone
I return to my troubled silence.

Hope Has Bidden Me Farewell

Hope has bidden me farewell,
Reward I see none,
Pleasure does not know me,
I do not lack for sorrow;
Where most I desire joy
There grows my torment;
None except days of sadness
Ever dawn for me;
The clear light of the sun
Darkens before my eyes.
In me the anguish of love
Never slumbers, though its cure
Sleeps to forget the glory
Which my sufferings deserve.
Death keeps me company
And offers herself hourly
But if I say "Kill me,"
She vanishes instantly
Rather than put an end
To my miseries, alas for me!
And the sense of my suffering
Grows numb and faints away,
But yet my will is not weakened
With my faith to sustain it.

Girl with the Dark Hair

Girl with the dark hair
If you are asleep, be warned:
Half of our life is a dream
Which runs and slips by us,
As rapid in its flight
As a light sleep wakened,
As brief while we are young
As when age is upon us,
For the sad disclosure
Of our fleet career
When it would wake us comes
Late and avails us nothing.
Your youth and beauty are
No more than a new merchant,
Rich to be left poor
By the lapse of time;
A glory of the world
And a veil for the eyes
And chains for the feet
And fetters for the fingers;
A ground for hazards,
A midden of envy,
A butcher of men,
A famous thief of time.
When death has shuffled

Ugly and fair together
In the narrow sepulcher
The bones do not know each other.
And though the cyprus is higher
And the cedar more lovely, neither,
Burned into charcoal, is whiter
Than charcoal from the ash tree.
For in this woeful existence
Delight comes to us in dreams only
And distress and tribulation
When we are widest awake.
Dry autumn will consume
The flower of fresh April,
To unloved ivory
Turning your ebon hair.

Tirsis

"Where are you, my lady,
Untouched by my sorrow?
It is either unknown to you, lady,
Or else you are false and disloyal.
Once you took pity upon me
When my wounds were little,
Now when they are mortal
You are not moved at all.
How can you ease me in small things
And in great ones fail me?
For in the gravest dangers
Friendship is found out
And the crucible of truth
Is adversity.
What round of memory
Renders you deaf to my weeping?
I can remember (when sorrows
Will let me remember)
How, on an alder trunk
By the bank of the Tagus,
When I was more fortunate
And you were more constant and true,
You wrote, with your hand, one day:
'I give you my liberty.
The Tagus will leave its bed

Before I turn from you.'
Roll back your water, river,
For faith departs from its word."
Such was the theme of Tirsis
As he sang alone
Memories of his lady,
Proofs of his sorrow.

Oh Pale Maiden

Oh pale maiden,
Sadness has faded
The rose of your face
In the April of your days.
All the village wonders
At such melancholy;
Such suffering, they say,
Is of the soul, not the body.
If such is your condition,
If your bewitching eyes
Which once killed with joy
Are now dead with sadness,
If you never go out to the dancing,
And to you the tambourine
Sounds like a knell tolling
And a bell at a burying,
If when all the girls
Go out into the fields
For cresses and to plunder
The young almonds of their kernels
You remain in your little house
In a lightless room
So that even when the sun shines
You are clouded over,
Who will fail to say

That you suffer on your left side
And are little seen because
You merit no better acquaintance,
That I leave you and seek my pleasure
Where I have none,
Often stealing away
In scorn of quiet nights,
That I ill-treat your soul
And that you are worse to your body
Since to purge it of love
You dose it with desire?
Come awake, my girl,
Wake out of your deep silence,
For the village speaks ill of me
And so do your father's eyes.
I have green slippers waiting for you
For the day when you set
Your fair foot on the floor,
And my mouth awaits you.
A little gown of light crimson
Will cover your body
Which more than four covet
As do I, who possess it.
You will have earrings of crystal
Which I pray you not to break
For words are of crystal, and those
Which I give I do not break.
And if still you will not recover

Your health, you for whom I lose mine,
Then give me the illness, my lady,
Or let us share it between us,
For if you must be ill I would rather
That I were the sufferer;
Not you, who are my soul,
But I, who am your body.

That Village Beauty

That village beauty
From the plain of Madrid
With the eyes dark and unsmiling,
Her waist and her body graceful,
She who knows of my torments
And is pleased to behold them,
Not so that she may restore me
But merely to watch me dying,
From a little mountain of roses,
Orange blossom and balm gentle,
She sallied forth to steal hearts
In the April mornings.

vi. A Wonder-mongering *Romance*

A Rare and Miraculous Case

You gentlemen lend me your ears
And do not be amazed,
And all you timid women,
Do not take fright at this:
It came to pass in Ireland,
As is true beyond a question,
That there was a poor woman
Who went to ask for alms,
She had many children with her,
They were beautiful to see;
She came to beg for money,
To provide them all with food,
From Doña Margarita,
A princess, as they say,
Without peer in that country.
When she saw so many children
She asked that poor soul:
"Are all those your own children?"
And she was answered thus:
"Yes, my lady, by one father,
Who's still living, at your service."
"Impossible," she answered,
"For I am very certain
That they're children of many fathers
As you cannot deny."

The poor soul was afflicted
At being slandered so,
She raised her hands to heaven
And kneeled down on the ground,
And she said: "Oh may it please God,
Who can do it if He will,
To send you so many children,
My lady, by one father,
That you won't know one from the others,
Nor be able to bring them up!"
This prayer was so acceptable
That that lady brought to birth
Three hundred and sixty children;
It was indeed a marvel!
They were all born in a single day
In pain, but with no danger,
Like little mice, they were so small,
And alive without exception.
And in a font of silver,
And by a bishop, they
Were every single one baptized,
And afterwards they went to taste
The glory which has no compare
Beyond all estimation.
That very font unto this day
In a church has been preserved,
And it was put upon display
To Charles our emperor.

And authors of great merit
To the truth of this will swear,
One is Baptista Fulgoso,
And Enrico, with Algozar,
And Doctor Vives of Valencia,
Who is not to be ignored.

Appendix: Introduction to 1961 Editions

The English word "ballad" is the closest we can get to the Spanish poems called *romances*. "Ballads" suggests a different metrical form, of course, and a different literary history. The *romances* are, and have been, even more central and important in Hispanic culture than the ballads are to the literary heritage of English.

In Spanish the *romances* grew so naturally out of the decay of the Spanish popular epic poetry that it is hard to say whether some of the oldest *romances* are separate poems from more or less complete cycles, or fragments of lost epics. For several centuries, throughout all of Spain and the Spanish-speaking world the *romances* were a kind of universal poetry, remembered, repeated, and composed by unlearned and by literate poets alike. They exerted an important influence on the rest of Spanish poetry: many of the lyric forms of the great age of Spanish literature show their *romance* parentage very plainly. The process worked the other way around too, and the *romance* tradition absorbed and reshaped a number of popular lyric forms as they fell into decadence. In the development of the Spanish drama the *romance* tradition was crucial. Some of the playwrights of the Golden Age simply dramatized events and stories which had already been shaped, developed, and sometimes in great part invented, over the course of several hundred years, by the thousands of imaginations through which the *romances* had passed. And the chief verse form of the Spanish classical drama—light, rapid, flexible, capable of great elegance or of colloquial abruptness without apparent strain—again bears a marked family resemblance to the main verse form of the *romances.* As for Spanish prose literature, there is no need to persuade anyone who has read *Don Quixote* that the *romances* were real and present to Cervantes, as they were to other novelists of his time. The music and the content of the *romances* pervade much of the imaginative literature of the great ages of Spain. The Spanish Golden Age and the last age of the *romances* ended virtually together.

But if they ended as literature the *romances* began as something else. From some indeterminate period before the twelfth century until late in the fifteenth the Iberian peninsula (and France and other parts of Europe) supported wandering performers who were responsible for the rise of one of the main poetic traditions in several of the countries where they flourished. The Spanish name for these professional performers was *juglares,* a word which (like the French *jongleur* and ultimately the English "juggler") comes from the Latin word *ioculari*—jokes—or *ioculator*—someone who entertains a crowd or a king by making them laugh: a joker, a clown. How the *juglares* themselves came into being is no longer known, but the generally accepted theory is that they derived from the wandering street entertainers of Rome and that their development was influenced by the bards and minstrels of the barbarian peoples. They are known to have existed in Spain by the seventh century, but it is not until the twelfth that they emerge into history as purveyors and fabricators of epic poetry.

In its heyday the word *juglar* was used more or less indiscriminately to describe people as different as the *trovadores* or literate poets (who eventually, in several of the Romance languages but most notably in Occitan, the language also known as Provencal, which survives as common speech in present-day Catalan, evolved a lyric tradition of great freshness, originality, and beauty) and the clowns who went around with performing monkeys. Not everyone remained happy about this easygoing nomenclature. The *trovadores* came to consider themselves not only superior to the rest of the *juglares* but also separate from them; some of them made it clear that they *composed* but did not *perform* their verses. The first of the Occitan troubadours whose poems are still with us was Guilhem de Peiteus, Count of Poitiers and Duke of Aquitaine, one of the most powerful noblemen in feudal France. But the individual fortunes of troubadours and of *trovadores* were not always so comfortable, and some of the *trovadores* sank to the position of wandering minstrels, which was what the *juglares*, properly speaking, were. The *juglares* (in this more precise sense of the word) sang and recited the epic *cantares*; they might be accompanied in their performances by mimes, known as *remendadores*, and *cazurros*—a name which included clowns and most varieties of stuntmen.

The *trovadores*, socially and politically, were drawn in two directions—on the one hand toward becoming court poets and developing a special poetry to fit courtly circumstances, and on the other toward the popular tradition and supplying narrative verse to the *juglares*, who would pay for it in order to make a living with it. The second of these two impulses was the older, and it is the one which concerns the origins of the *romances*.

For their sources *trovadores* relied upon such material as

Carolingian history and legends, or the history and legends of Spain: the life and triumphs of the Cid, for example, or of Fernán-González, or the tragic stories of King Don Rodrigo, "the last of the Goths," or Bernardo del Carpio, or the Seven Princes of Lara. And they adapted the stories of classical antiquity or the Bible. There is no doubt that there were complete *cantares,* as full and finished as *El Cantar del Mio Cid,* dealing with these and many other subjects, but none of them has survived except in fragments or in prose transcripts in later chronicles.

The verse in which the epic *cantares* was composed looks like this when written down (the passage is from *The Poem of the Cid*):

> De los sos ojos   tan fuertemientre llorando,
> tornava la cabeca   i estávalos catando.
> Vió puertas abiertas   e ucos sin canados,
> alcándaras vazias   sin pieles e sin mantos
> e sin falcones   e sin adtores mudados.

> (From his eyes   bitterly weeping,
> He turned his head   and stayed looking back at them.
> He saw doors standing open   and gates without fastenings,
> The racks empty   without furs and without mantles
> And without falcons   and without mewed goshawks.)

Scholars have spent much time and argument in trying to establish the rules upon which this kind of verse was written and what its sources are, and at last have virtually agreed that it was for the most part, at least, an indigenous Spanish form and that there was no rigid metrical or syllabic pattern to which the poets were trying to conform. Rather, the verse, mechanically speaking, was a relatively free form which the *trovadores* played by ear and adapted to the needs of their narrative. Still, it is possible to make a few generalizations. The epic *cantares* were composed in a long flexible line with a marked break somewhere in the middle. The nearest equivalent in the English tradition is the Middle English line in which *Piers Plowman* is written. However, the Spanish line does not have the regular accentual pattern of the Middle English verse, nor its alliterative scheme. At least in historical theory it tends to a normal length of sixteen syllables. The lines end not in rhyme but in an assonance pattern. In the passage quoted above, the last two syllables of each line are the vowels *a-o:* llor*a*nd*o*, cant*a*nd*o*, can*a*d*o*s, etc. An assonance pattern of this kind can run on for a hundred lines or more, or may change after five or six.

The latter part of the fourteenth century saw the decline of the epic tradition in Spain. Not only did the sources themselves dry up, from causes and at a time which are both largely unknown to history, but also the existing poems were sung less and less often, and gradually, since they had not been written down, were lost. But not entirely. Isolated episodes, situations, descriptions, characters, refrains would be remembered, repeated, and sung, in private, for the pleasure of it. They would retain the sound and the formal elements of the lost epics. Gradually they began to take on a shape and completeness of their own, and the *romances* were born.

They can be (and occasionally, for reasons of space, they are) printed to look like the verse of the epic *cantares;* but it is more usual to treat the halves of the old line as two separate lines, so that a passage of a *romance* usually looks like this:

> Ya se partia el buen Cid
> sin al rey besar la mano;
> ya se parte de sus tierras,
> de Vivar y sus palacios:
> las puertas deja cerradas,
> los alamudes echados,
> las cadenas deja llenas
> de podencos y de galgos;
> solo lleva sus falcones,
> los pollos y los mudados.

> (Now the good Cid has gone
> Without kissing the King's hand;
> Now he goes from his lands,
> From Vivar and its palaces:
> He leaves the doors closed
> And the bolts fastened,
> He leaves on their chains
> The hounds and the grayhounds,
> He takes only his falcons,
> The fledglings and the mewed birds.)

This passage and the one from *The Poem of the Cid* describe the same departure. The differences in the two narratives are obvious, but the two passages, at different stages of the same tradition, are, formally, virtually the same. The *romance,* however, is more regular; the lines keep closer to their norm of eight syllables each, and the rhythm is more regular than in the older poem. The assonance pattern remains (m*a*no, pal*a*cio, esch*a*dos, etc.), and the rhythm still runs in units of two lines, every two lines corresponding to one line in the old *cantares*. As the *romances* moved further and further away from their epic origins the pause at the end of the second line sometimes grew fainter. In some of the literary *romances* of the seventeenth century the assonances are virtually all that is left to recall this element of the old rhythmic scheme. However, the pause pattern was never lost in the popular literature and is still unmistakably there in traditional *romances* collected in Spain and South America in this century. This unbroken connection with the indigenous popular epics of the Middle Ages is one thing which makes the Spanish *romances* unique among the ballad literatures of the rest of Europe.

As might have been expected, in the period of the decay of the *cantares* the parts of the epics which were usually remembered were those in which a single situation stood out in intense relief against a background of historical or legendary narrative. In the *romances* the purely narrative elements were gradually reduced, simplified, or merely lost, and more and more emphasis came to be placed on the lyrical development of a situation.

One of the distinct characteristics of the Spanish *cantares,* in comparison with the French *chansons de geste* and other popular epics of the Middle Ages, had been a capacity for dealing with contemporary, or nearly contemporary, experience. *The Poem of the Cid* was written only forty-some years after the death of its hero, and from what evidence remains it seems likely that some of the other Spanish epics dealt with historical events which were no further removed from the period in which they were first sung. The *romances* carried on this tradition. Until the genre degenerated into a merely literary imitation of its former self there were *romances* which narrated the battles, the memorable events, the lives and deaths of the great figures of their own times. Of course ballads of this kind are common in other literatures too, but Spain is particularly rich in this kind of historical poetry.

Early in their development, Spanish *romances* came to include the simple, single-episode stories which one immediately thinks of when ballads are mentioned. Some of these stories—the identical situations—can be found in many of the ballad literatures of Europe. There is, for instance, the universally popular story of the adulterous wife whose vengeful husband visits her in the guise of her lover, in *The Mistress of Bernal Francés*. This poem is a good example, too, of the economy and dramatic precision which abound in the *romances*. The richness of descriptive detail heightens the suspense in a situation whose outcome, as the reader is made to feel at the beginning, cannot fail to be tragic; and the echo of these descriptions in the husband's quiet and deadly promises to his wife add to the feeling of terror at the end of the poem. This *romance* illustrates another characteristic of these Spanish poems: in comparison with most other ballad literatures, the *romances* are deliberately abrupt and apparently fragmentary. It became virtually a convention to develop a situation until its consequences were just visible and then stop short rather than describe them.

One theory suggests that the taste for this kind of conclusion was a result of the genuinely fragmentary nature of the early *romances*. But it is also true that this love of concision and implication rather than elaboration runs through much of Spanish popular poetry. It can be found, for instance, in the very short, compressed forms of the popular lyric such as the *copla* and the *estribillo*.

The seven hundred years' war with the Moors was one of the chief formative experiences in the history and culture of Spain. One of its more obvious effects upon Spanish literature was the creation of a kind of *romance* which narrates the experiences of war, love, captivity, or whatever it may be, from a Moorish, or at least a fictitiously Moorish, point of view. There are several of these *romances* in this selection.

The Jewish population of Spain, on the other hand, developed a rich, intense poetry in its own Spanish-Jewish dialect, including a body of *romances;* some of these are included also. Not only Castilian but all of the Romance languages of the Iberian Peninsula can boast large numbers of *romances* even today, many of them variants of well-known poems which exist in Castilian, but some are to be found nowhere else. "The Corpse-keeper" and "One Castle, Two Castles" are from Catalán, not Castilian, originals.

During the sixteenth and seventeenth centuries the *romance* underwent several changes. *Romances* were composed by cultivated poets who wrote in other forms as well. They were used for satire, for verse epistles, for epigrams and epitaphs which assumed no narrative context at all. Some of the new *romances* gave utterance to the amorous elegiac laments of the same shepherds and shepherdesses who recur throughout the Renaissance literature of Europe. These *romances* are more lyric and meditative, less narrative or dramatic than the older, traditional ones. I have included poems which illustrate these latter developments of the form, and also an example of those (relatively late) *romances* which vouched for the veracity of marvels and prodigies, a popular convention that Shakespeare knew and relayed in the lines of Autolycus about

> a fish that appeared upon the coast on Wednesday the fourscore of April, forty thousand fathom above water, and sung this ballad against the hard hearts of maids. It was thought she was a woman...

There were English wonder-mongering ballads such as the one which, most wonderful of all, was true, about the Genoese Siamese twins, John Baptist and Lazarus Colloretti, of whom it was established at the start that

> ...a Gentleman well qualifide
> Doth bear his brother at his side
> Inseparably knit.

All of the *romances* in the present selection are anonymous, which makes dating them, and consequently any kind of chronological arrangement, very difficult. The date when a poem was first written down of course tells nothing about the date of its composition, and scholarship has to rely on internal evidence to determine the age of many *romances*. I have arranged the poems in groups starting with the early legendary and historical cycles and ending with the marvel-mongering piece: this method of presenting them is in fact very roughly chronological, but its only real virtue is convenience.

It would be far from correct to call the language of the *romances* "natural," since it is the result of a highly developed poetic convention and of loving artifice, but it is simple, direct, precise. At its best it seems both inevitable and unexpected. These qualities, and the literal sense of the poems, are what I have tried to evoke in English. In some *romances,* particularly in the earlier ones which evolved directly from the *cantares,* the use of the present and past tenses differs considerably from that of modern English, or modern Spanish, for that matter. It has been suggested that, at least in the epics themselves, the present tense was used to bring a scene or a detail into the foreground, and the past tenses to give the effect of distance whether in time or space. In translating the poems I have for the most part preferred to alter the tenses as little as possible unless that sounded hopelessly awkward or confusing in English. It seemed to me that in retaining, as a general rule, the same use of tenses as the originals, the translations were brought a shade closer to the Spanish poems. On the other hand, I have made no attempt to match the assonance patterns or the originals with English rhymes. Rhyme does not come as naturally to English as assonances do to Spanish, especially in cases where sets of thirty or forty rhymes on one sound might be called for. Some approximation to the assonances of the originals would of course have been possible, but it would inevitably have involved distortion of language and a certain clogging of rhythm. My aim was not to produce a series of virtuoso performances but a group of translations which would be faithful and readable, and would get in the way of the originals as little as possible.

I wish to express my gratitude to Mr. P. Harvey of Queen Mary College, University of London, for helping me with some of the problems of translation, and to the Hispanic Council and its librarians for their patient generosity.

W.S. Merwin
London
January 1960
(Revised January 2008)

Bibliography and Notes

The most important modern student of the *romances* is Don Ramon Menéndez Pidal. Anyone who takes pleasure in these poems and tries to find out something about them falls rapidly into his debt. Not only has he collected them himself for years, but also his works on the tradition of the *romances*—their origin, their place in the life of the people who made them and who handed them down from generation to generation, their development, their variation, their distribution, etc.—have contributed enormously to the modern interest in and understanding of the *romances*. For readers who know Spanish, his large volume on the *Romancero Español,* his *Poesía Juglaresca y Juglares,* and his *De Primitiva Lírica Española y Antigua Épica* are standard works, authoritative, and rich in information, and the last two at least are easily obtainable (in the *Colección Austral*).

The collections from which I have made these translations are the following:

1. *Flor Nueva de Romances Viejos*—Ramon Menéndez Pidal, Colección Austral—Buenos Aires—Espasa Calpe. 1948.

2. *Romancero Español*—por Luis Santuellano, Selección de Romances Antiguos y Modernos, Según las Coleccíones Más Autorizadas. Aguilar, Madrid. 1946.

3. *Romancero General*—Colección de Romances Castellanos Anteriores al Siglo XVIII—por Don Agustín Duran—2 volumes—Biblioteca de Autores Españoles—Madrid. 1945.

4. *Romancero Popular de la Montaña*—Colección de Romances Tradicionales Recogido y Ordenados por José María de Cossio y Tomás Maza Solano—Sociedad Menéndez y Pelayo—Librería Moderna, Santander.

5. *Romances de Tradición Oral*—José M. de Cossio—Colección Austral—Espasa Calpe, Buenos Aires.

6. *Anthología de Poesía Española*—by Damaso Alonso y J.M. Blecua.

7. *Romancero del Cid*—M.E. Aguilar—Colección Criso—Madrid. 1944.

There are also selections of the *romances* in the *Oxford Book of Spanish Verse* and in the *Penguin Book of Spanish Verse,* the latter accompanied by prose translations.

For those who may want to use the present versions in order to get closer to the original poems I append a list of textual sources for these. Where the same text occurs in several collections I have mentioned the most easily available one. In the list the collections which I have named are referred to as follows:

FN   *Flor Nueva de Romances Viejos*
RE   *Romancero Español*
RG   *Romancero General*
RM   *Romancero Popular de la Montaña*
RTO   *Romances de Tradición Oral*
APE   *Anthología de Poesía Española*
OB   *Oxford Book of Spanish Verse*
RC   *Romancero del Cid*

The first number in each case refers to the poem's number in the Table of Contents of this volume.

1. FN (As the pagination of this collection and of the *Romancero General* has changed from printing to printing, I have not given page numbers for the poems from these collections.)
2. RE, variant FN
3. FN
4. FN
5. FN
6. FN
7. RE
8. FN
9. FN
10. RE
11. FN
12. FN
13. RC p. 466
14. RE, FN
15. OB p. 72
16. OB p. 65
17. RE
18. FN
19. OB p. 71, FN
20. composite of variants in FN and RE

21. RE

22. RE

23. RE

24. OB p. 65

25. FN

26. OB p. 70, variant FN

27. many variants; OB p. 73, FN, and others in other collections

28. OB p. 71

29. OB p. 70

30. FN (a variant: OB p.72)

31. RE

32. RE

33. RE

34. RE

35. RE

36. RE

37. RE

38. RG vol. 2 p. 214

39. FN

40. APE p. 4

41. RE

42. RG vol. 2 p. 450

43. RTO p. 130

44. RE

45. RE

46. RE

47. RG vol. 2 p. 215

48. RE

49. RE

50. RE, OB p. 59

51. FN

52. RE

53. OB p. 69, variant FN

54. FN

55. RM

56. RE

57. OB p. 63, FN

58. RG vol. 2 p. 89

59. OB p. 64, FN

60. RE

61. OB p. 64

62. RE

63. RG vol. 2 p. 119

64. RG vol. 2 p. 448

65. RG vol. 2 p. 491

66. RG vol. 2 p. 431

67. RG vol. 2 p. 419

68. RG vol. 2 p. 487

69. RG vol. 2

70. RG vol. 2 p. 508

71. RG vol. 2 p. 393

About the Translator

W.S. Merwin was born in New York City in 1927. From 1949 to 1951, he worked as a tutor in France, Majorca, and Portugal; for several years afterward he made the greater part of his living by translating from French, Spanish, Latin, and Portuguese. His many awards include the Pulitzer Prize in Poetry, the Lannan Lifetime Achievement Award, the Tanning Prize for mastery in the art of poetry (now the Wallace Stevens Award), the Bollingen Award, the Ruth Lilly Poetry Prize, the Bobbitt National Prize for Poetry, as well as fellowships from the Rockefeller and the Guggenheim foundations and the National Endowment for the Arts. He is the author of many books of poetry and prose; his most recent volumes of poems are *Migration: New & Selected Poems,* winner of the National Book Award, and *Present Company.* For the past thirty years he has lived in Hawaii.

The Chinese character for poetry is made up of two parts: "word" and "temple." It also serves as pressmark for Copper Canyon Press.

Since 1972, Copper Canyon Press has fostered the work of emerging, established, and world-renowned poets for an expanding audience. The Press thrives with the generous patronage of readers, writers, booksellers, librarians, teachers, students, and funders—everyone who shares the belief that poetry is vital to language and living.

Major funding has been provided by:

Anonymous (2)

Sarah and Tim Cavanaugh

Beroz Ferrell & The Point, LLC

Lannan Foundation

National Endowment for the Arts

Cynthia Lovelace Sears and Frank Buxton

Washington State Arts Commission

For information and catalogs:

COPPER CANYON PRESS
Post Office Box 271
Port Townsend, Washington 98368
360-385-4925
www.coppercanyonpress.org

Copper Canyon Classics re-presents essential, formative poetry texts in
an affordable format. This book is set in Legacy Serif, a font designed
by American type designer Ronald Arnholm after close study of
Nicholas Jenson's 1470 Eusebius. Display type set in Reminga
Titling, designed by Xavier Dupré. Book design and
composition by Valerie Brewster, Scribe Typography.
Printed at McNaughton and Gunn, Inc.

Copper Canyon
Classics